HIDDEN HEROES FROM A TO Z

Hidden History Museum
2023 King Flex Entertainment

Copyright 2023

KING FLEX ENT.

WWW.HIDDENHISTORYMUSEUM.COM

No part of this publication may be copied, distributed, or transmitted in any form or by any means, including photocopying, recording, or other electronic or mechanical methods, without the prior written permission of the publisher, except in the case of brief quotations embodied in reviews and specific other non-commercial uses permitted by copyright law.

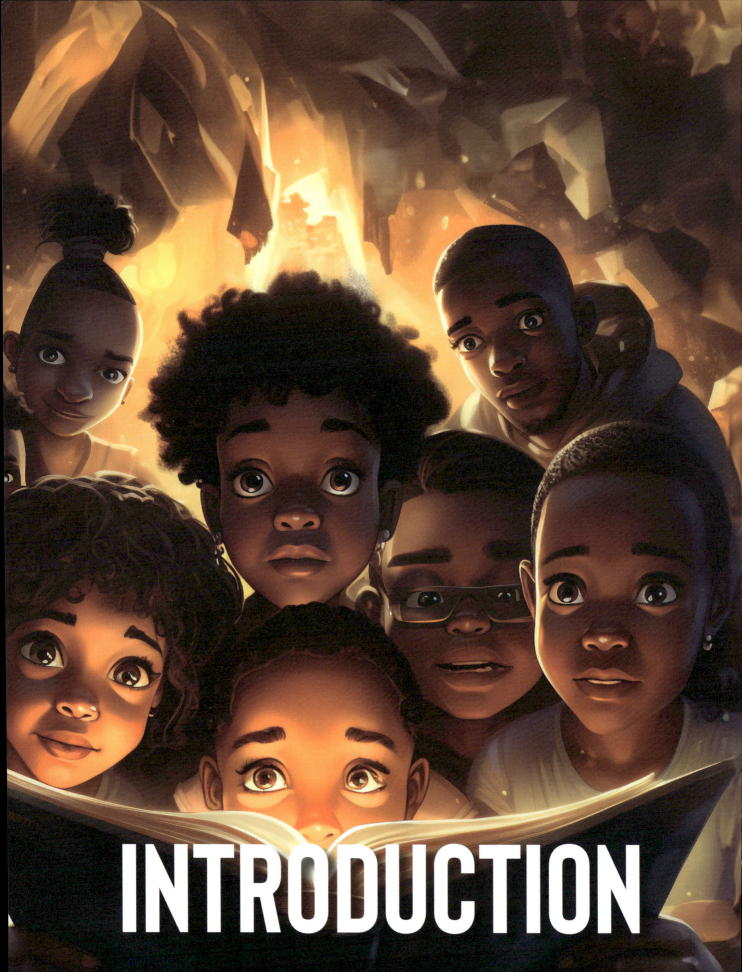

INTRODUCTION

INTRODUCTION

Welcome to the extraordinary world of "Hidden Heroes From A to Z"! Within the vibrant pages of this book, we embark on a captivating journey that celebrates the remarkable Black heroes who have shaped history. From well-known figures to unsung champions, this book will shed light on their inspiring stories through brief biographies and fascinating factoids.

Geared towards young readers, "Hidden Heroes From A to Z" invites children and young adults to discover the diverse and often overlooked contributions of Black heroes. However, readers of all ages, young and old, will find this book an enriching and enlightening experience.

Each page of this captivating volume unravels the narratives of these exceptional individuals, sharing their triumphs, struggles, and enduring legacies. Through colorful illustrations and engaging text, readers will be transported to moments of bravery, resilience, and groundbreaking achievements.

From courageous activists who fought for justice, to visionary artists who transformed the creative landscape, to brilliant scientists who pushed the boundaries of knowledge, this book showcases the breadth and depth of Black excellence across various fields.

"Hidden Heroes From A to Z" is not just an educational resource; it is a celebration of the extraordinary human spirit. It aims to inspire young minds, foster a sense of pride and identity, and encourage readers to embrace the dignity of our shared history.

So, join us on this enlightening journey as we honor the incredible contributions of Black heroes. Their stories deserve to be known, cherished, and celebrated by all.

MUHAMMAD ALI

MUHAMMAD ALI
(1942-2016) A Boxing Legend's Journey

Muhammad Ali, born Cassius Marcellus Clay Jr. on January 17, 1942, is widely regarded as one of the greatest boxers of all time. His remarkable career, filled with triumphs and challenges, left an indelible mark on the sport and the world at large.

Ali's ascent in the boxing world began in his hometown of Louisville, Kentucky. His talent for boxing became evident at an early age, leading him to win a gold medal at the 1960 Olympics in Rome. Blessed with lightning-fast footwork, powerful punches, and an unmatched charisma, Ali quickly became a household name.

However, his journey was not without its share of controversy. In 1964, Ali announced his conversion to the Nation of Islam, a religious and political movement advocating for the rights of Black Americans. Changing his name to Muhammad Ali, he embraced his new faith, which played a significant role in shaping his identity and beliefs.

At the height of his fame and success, Ali faced a pivotal moment that would define his legacy. In 1967, he refused to be drafted into the U.S. military for the Vietnam War. Ali cited his religious beliefs and opposition to the war as the reasons behind his refusal. This courageous stand cost him his boxing titles and led to a five-year ban from the sport.

During his exile from boxing, Ali focused on activism and speaking engagements, advocating for peace and civil rights. In 1971, the Supreme Court overturned his conviction, allowing him to return to the ring. Ali's comeback was nothing short of extraordinary as he reclaimed his heavyweight championship title in a historic bout against George Foreman in 1974. This victory, known as the "Rumble in the Jungle," solidified his place as one of boxing's all-time greats.

Aside from his boxing prowess, Ali's life was filled with other noteworthy moments:

1. In 1981, Ali demonstrated his compassion and bravery when he talked a suicidal man off the ledge of a building. His words of empathy and understanding saved a life, showcasing his humanity and genuine concern for others.
2. In 1990, during the Gulf War, Ali traveled to Iraq and played a vital role in negotiating the release of 15 American hostages held captive by Saddam Hussein's regime. His

diplomatic efforts and personal rapport with the Iraqi leadership resulted in the safe return of the hostages.

Muhammad Ali's legacy extends far beyond his accomplishments in the ring. He was an iconic figure who used his platform to advocate for peace, racial justice, and humanitarian causes. Ali's charisma, sharp wit, and unwavering principles continue to inspire individuals of all ages.

MAYA ANGELOU

(1928-2014): A Trailblazing Voice of Resilience

Maya Angelou, born Marguerite Annie Johnson on April 4, 1928, was a renowned poet, author, and civil rights activist. Throughout her impactful career, Angelou left an indelible mark on literature and society, using her words to empower and inspire. Let's delve into some significant facts about Maya Angelou's extraordinary life and achievements.

Angelou's successful writing career spanned across various genres, encompassing poetry, memoirs, essays, and even screenplays. Her debut memoir, "I Know Why the Caged Bird Sings," published in 1969, received critical acclaim and became a literary classic. This deeply personal work explored themes of racial identity, trauma, and resilience, resonating with readers worldwide.

In addition to her literary achievements, Maya Angelou's talent as a spoken word artist was recognized with several Grammy Awards. She won a total of three Grammys in the Best Spoken Word Album category, showcasing her ability to captivate audiences through the power of her voice and storytelling.

Remarkably, Maya Angelou's works have also faced controversy and censorship. She is among the most banned authors in America, with her books often challenged due to their honest depictions of sensitive topics, including racism and violence. Despite these challenges, Angelou's writings continue to inspire readers and foster important conversations about social issues.

Angelou's accomplishments extended beyond writing. In 1972, she became the first Black woman to write a screenplay for a major motion picture, "Georgia, Georgia." This groundbreaking achievement broke barriers in the film industry, highlighting her versatility and pioneering spirit.

Maya Angelou's legacy is one of resilience, activism, and poetic brilliance. Her eloquent words and powerful storytelling illuminated the experiences of Foundational Black Americans, and shed light on the human capacity for strength and triumph over adversity.

BENJAMIN BANNEKER

BENJAMIN BANNEKER

(1731-1806): A Trailblazer in Science and Design

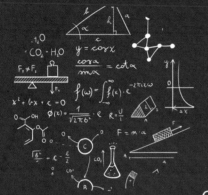

Benjamin Banneker, born on November 9, 1731, was an extraordinary individual whose thirst for knowledge and innovative thinking left a lasting impact. Let's explore the captivating story of Benjamin Banneker, from his early life to his remarkable accomplishments.

During his early years, Banneker grew up on a farm in Maryland. Although he was born into a time when educational opportunities for Black individuals were limited, his family valued learning and encouraged his intellectual growth. Determined to educate himself, young Benjamin Banneker taught himself how to read and write. Through hard work and perseverance, he developed a strong foundation for his future endeavors.

Banneker's curiosity extended to various fields, and his passion for astronomy and mathematics led him to create his almanacs. These almanacs were detailed compilations of astronomical calculations, weather predictions, and practical advice. Banneker dedicated hours to researching and meticulously organizing data to provide valuable information to farmers, sailors, and curious minds. His almanacs, starting in 1792, became highly regarded resources, showcasing his keen intellect and dedication to sharing knowledge.

In addition to his interest in astronomy and almanacs, Benjamin Banneker displayed remarkable skills in clockmaking. Inspired by a pocket watch he borrowed, he sought to construct his own timekeeping device. Through careful study and experimentation, Banneker crafted a fully functional wooden clock, which ran accurately for many years. His talent for clockmaking demonstrated his ability to blend mathematical principles with craftsmanship.

Here are five other rarely known factoids about Benjamin Banneker:

1. Banneker was also an accomplished farmer and implemented innovative agricultural techniques on his land.
2. He corresponded with Thomas Jefferson, challenging Jefferson's views on racial equality and advocating for equal rights for all.
3. Banneker's mathematical expertise allowed him to accurately predict solar and lunar eclipses.

4. He was an abolitionist, speaking out against slavery and writing powerful letters denouncing its inhumanity.

5. Banneker was known for his musical abilities and played the violin, contributing to his multifaceted talents.

It is believed that Benjamin Banneker may be descended from the Dogon tribe of Africa, a tribe recognized for its advanced astronomical knowledge. This ancestral connection adds depth to Banneker's fascination with the cosmos and his understanding of celestial phenomena.

Benjamin Banneker's involvement in the design and architecture of Washington DC is a topic of great significance and debate. While his contributions are often minimized, many historians believe that Banneker played a crucial role in shaping the city's layout and design. In fact, some speculate that he may be the true architect of Washington DC. The commotion surrounding Banneker's involvement raises important questions about the erasure of Black contributions in history and the lingering effects of anti-Black racism. Recognizing and celebrating Banneker's influence on the nation's capital sheds light on the immense talents and intellect of Foundational Black Americans and challenges the narratives that have historically marginalized their achievements.

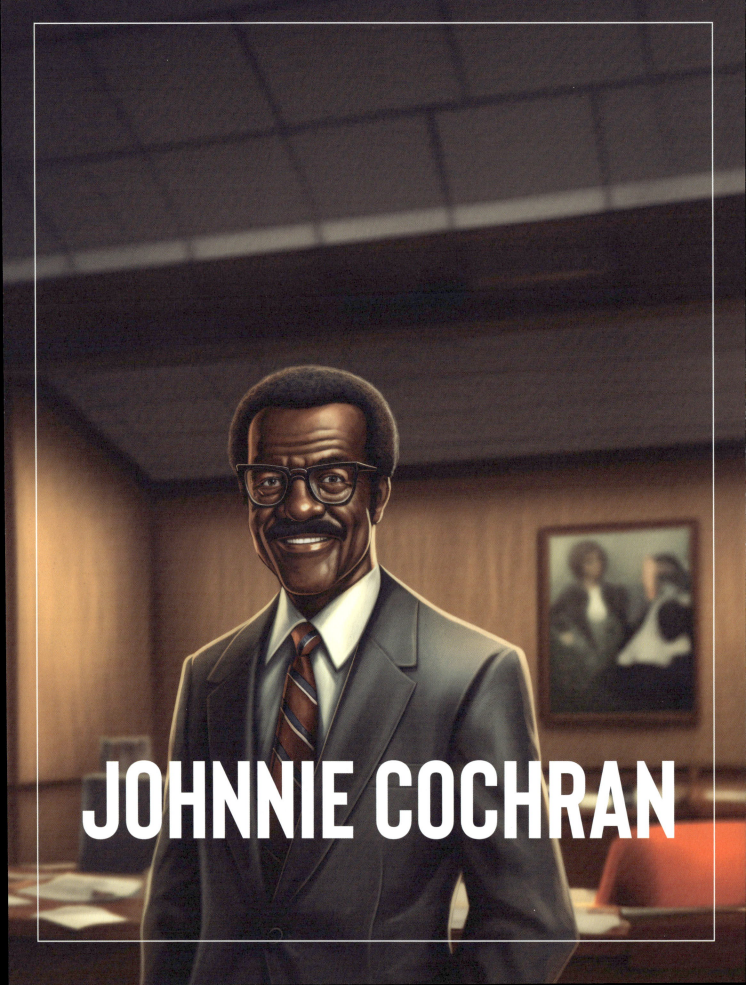

JOHNNIE COCHRAN

(1937-2005): The Fearless Champion of Justice

Johnnie Cochran, born on October 2, 1937, was a prominent lawyer whose passion for justice and exceptional courtroom skills propelled him to become one of the most renowned figures in American legal history.

Cochran's journey began in Shreveport, Louisiana, where he developed a deep sense of justice and equality from his parents. His pursuit of education led him to earn a law degree from the University of California, Los Angeles (UCLA). From the early stages of his career, Cochran exhibited a steadfast dedication to representing the underprivileged and those who faced systemic injustices.

Throughout his illustrious career, Johnnie Cochran represented numerous high-profile clients. Some of his most famous clients included Snoop Dogg, Michael Jackson, Tupac Shakur, Sean "Diddy" Combs, and Geronimo Pratt, among others. Cochran's courtroom prowess and unwavering commitment to his clients' rights earned him a reputation as a formidable advocate.

However, it was Cochran's involvement in the O.J. Simpson case that brought him international acclaim. In 1995, he joined Simpson's defense team, utilizing his exceptional legal skills and strategic thinking to craft a compelling defense. Cochran's masterful courtroom performance, along with his iconic phrase, "If it doesn't fit, you must acquit," captivated audiences worldwide and secured a not-guilty verdict for Simpson.

Beyond his renowned cases, Johnnie Cochran was dedicated to seeking justice for historical injustices. He had plans to pursue compensation for the survivors of the Tulsa Race Massacre, a tragic event in 1921 when a prosperous Black community in Tulsa, Oklahoma, was attacked and destroyed. Cochran also envisioned going to court to advocate for reparations for Foundational Black Americans, seeking to address the enduring effects of slavery and systemic racism through the legal system.

While Johnnie Cochran passed away on March 29, 2005, his legacy continues to resonate. His commitment to justice, his groundbreaking defense strategies, and his advocacy for reparations have left an indelible impact on the legal profession and society at large.

KATHRINE DUNHAM

KATHERINE DUNHAM

(1909-2006): The Matriarch and Queen Mother of Black Dance

Katherine Dunham, born on June 22, 1909, was a pioneering Black American dancer, choreographer, and anthropologist who left an indelible mark on the world of dance. Known as the Matriarch and Queen Mother of Black Dance, Dunham's innovative approach and cultural influence continue to resonate.

Dunham's unique choreographic style combined elements of African and Caribbean dance with modern Foundational Black American techniques, creating a vibrant and expressive form of movement. Her innovative fusion of diverse cultural traditions showcased the richness and beauty of Black dance. Due to her groundbreaking contributions, she earned the title of the Matriarch and Queen Mother of Black Dance, symbolizing her leadership and influence within the dance community.

Beyond her own accomplishments, Katherine Dunham's legacy also lies in her profound influence on other renowned dancers. Famed choreographer Alvin Ailey, among many others, was inspired by Dunham's pioneering work. Ailey acknowledged Dunham as his mentor and credited her with shaping his artistic vision and the establishment of the Alvin Ailey American Dance Theater, one of the most celebrated dance companies in the world. Dunham's impact extends to numerous other dancers who drew inspiration from her innovative techniques and commitment to cultural authenticity.

Throughout her career, Dunham broke down racial barriers in the dance world and fought against discrimination. She established the Katherine Dunham Dance Company, becoming the first Black American dance company to tour extensively in the United States and abroad. By showcasing the talent and artistic excellence of Black dancers, she shattered stereotypes and opened doors for future generations.

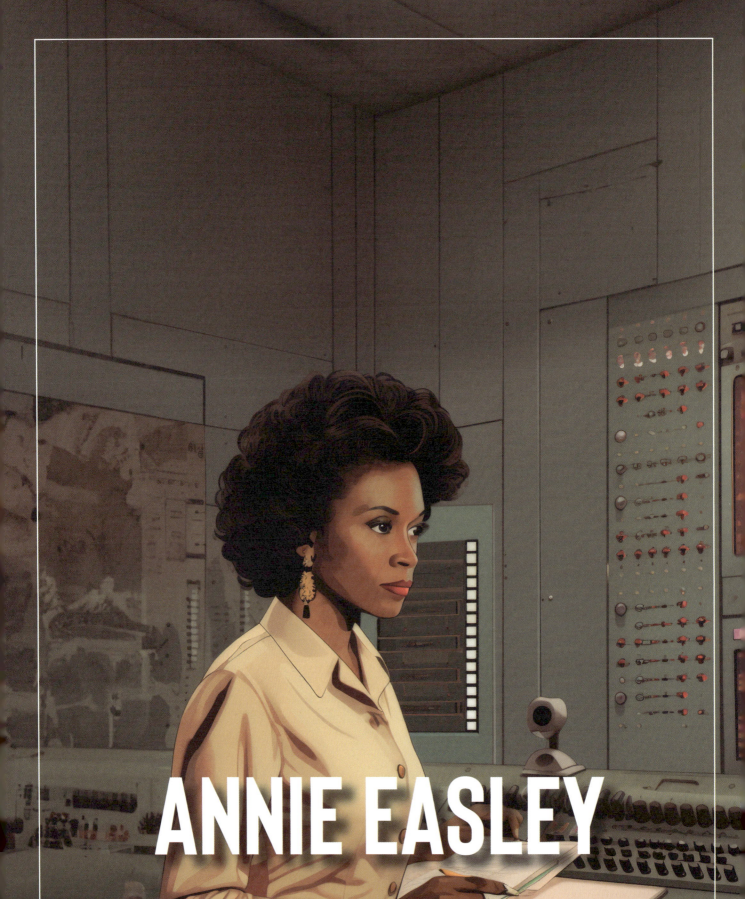

E

ANNIE EASLEY

(1933-2011): The Amazing Computer Scientist

Annie Easley, a remarkable Foundational Black American computer scientist, was born on April 23, 1933. Her incredible innovations and contributions to the world of computing have left a lasting impact.

Annie Easley was a trailblazer in computer programming and software development. She played a crucial role in the early days of computer science at the National Aeronautics and Space Administration (NASA). Her work helped propel the field forward and made a significant difference.

Here are some interesting facts about Annie Easley and her incredible achievements:

1. Easley worked on developing software for the Centaur rocket stage, which helped NASA in various space missions and explorations.

2. She used computer simulations to study alternative energy systems, such as wind and solar power, helping scientists find better ways to generate clean and renewable energy.

3. Easley was a problem-solver extraordinaire. She created software that calculated rocket trajectories, making sure they went in the right direction and reached their targets.

4. She was known as the "human computer" because of her exceptional mathematical skills and ability to solve complex problems quickly and accurately.

Annie Easley's contributions to computer science were remarkable. She believed in the power of computers to solve real-world problems and improve people's lives. Easley was passionate about making sure everyone had equal opportunities to succeed in the field of computer science.

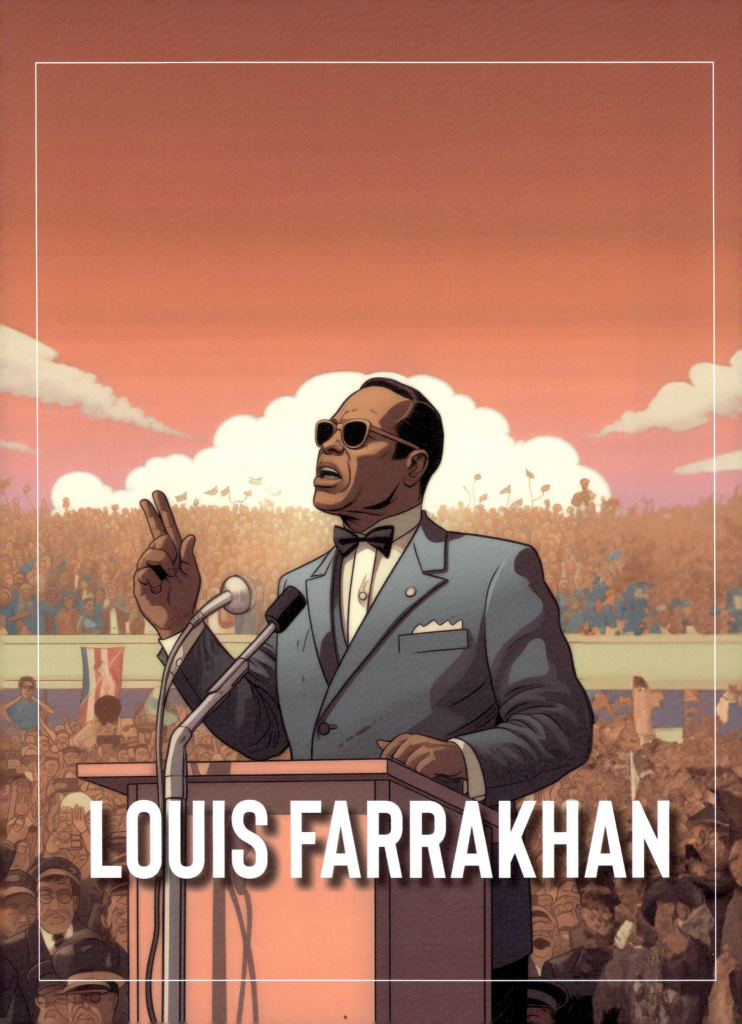

LOUIS FARRAKHAN

Louis Farrakhan (born Louis Eugene Walcott on May 11, 1933) is an influential religious leader known for his role as the leader of the Nation of Islam. Let's explore the life of Minister Louis Farrakhan, his beliefs, and his impact.

Minister Louis Farrakhan has been a prominent figure in American religious and social circles for many years. He joined the Nation of Islam in the 1950s and became a protégé of its leader, Elijah Muhammad. After Elijah Muhammad's death in 1975, Farrakhan assumed leadership of the organization.

Farrakhan's speeches and teachings have often focused on empowering and uplifting Black communities, promoting self-reliance, and addressing social issues such as racism and inequality. While he has faced criticism for some of his statements, particularly those perceived as controversial, Farrakhan has also been praised by his followers for his advocacy and commitment to the Black community.

One of the significant events associated with Minister Louis Farrakhan is the Million Man March, which took place in Washington, D.C., on October 16, 1995. This event brought together over one million Black men from different backgrounds to advocate for unity, self-improvement, and social change.

Minister Farrakhan's influence extends beyond religious and social activism. He has been involved in initiatives such as economic empowerment, promoting Black businesses, and fostering a sense of pride and cultural identity among his followers.

A.G GASTON

(1892-1996): The Black Business Titan

Arthur George Gaston, born on July 4, 1892, was an influential Foundational Black American businessman who played a significant role in shaping the business landscape and civil rights movement. Let's explore the remarkable life of A. G. Gaston, from his early years to his outstanding achievements.

Growing up in Demopolis, Alabama, A. G. Gaston experienced the challenges of racial segregation that prevailed during his time. However, he remained determined and sought opportunities to uplift himself and his community through entrepreneurship.

Gaston's business ventures spanned various industries, including insurance, real estate, banking, and funeral services. One of his most notable accomplishments was the establishment of the Booker T. Washington Insurance Company, which became one of the largest Black-owned insurance companies in the United States. He also owned a motel, a radio station, and other enterprises, all of which provided employment opportunities and economic empowerment to Black communities.

At the pinnacle of his success, A. G. Gaston became the wealthiest Black man in America. His remarkable journey from humble beginnings to extraordinary prosperity showcased his entrepreneurial skills, dedication, and hard work. Gaston's achievements served as an inspiration to others, demonstrating the potential for success regardless of one's background.

Apart from his business endeavors, A. G. Gaston actively participated in the civil rights movement. He utilized his influence and resources to support the fight for racial equality. One notable example of his activism was when he threatened to withdraw his funds from a local bank that displayed "whites only" signs. As a result, the bank promptly removed the discriminatory signs, marking a small but significant victory in the battle against segregation.

A. G. Gaston's life is a testament to the power of entrepreneurship and the pursuit of justice. His success as a businessman and his involvement in the civil rights movement highlight his enduring legacy.

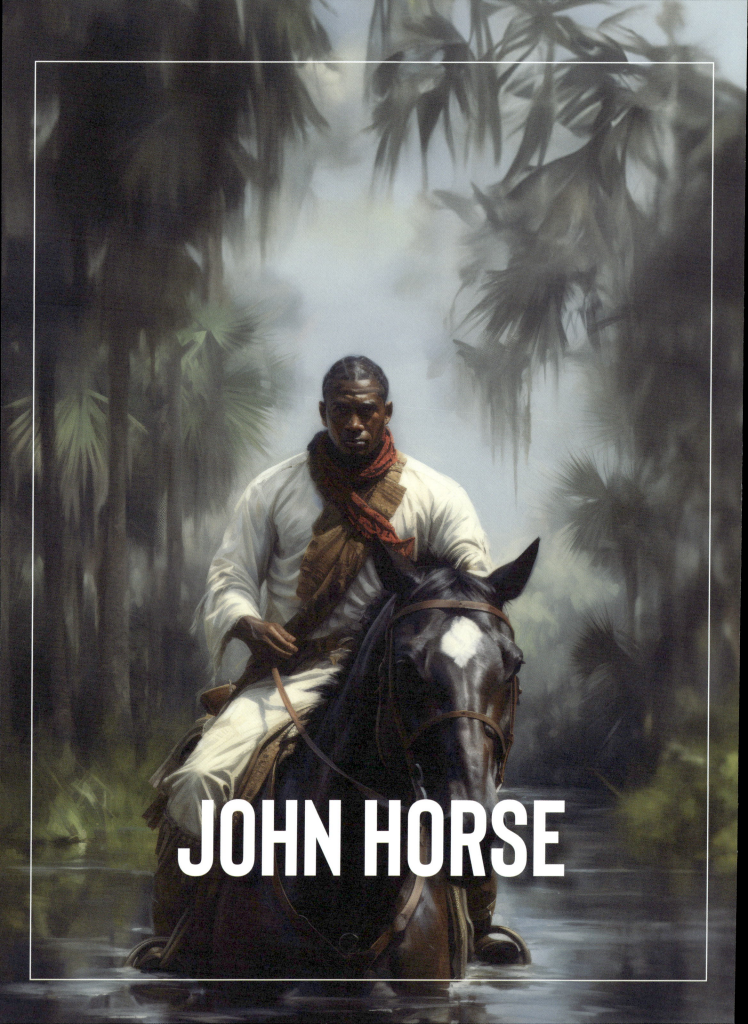

JOHN HORSE

(1812-1882): The Fearless Black Seminole Leader

John Horse, born in 1812, was an extraordinary Black Seminole leader who played a pivotal role in the fight against slavery in Florida and the defense of his people's freedom. Let's delve into the life of John Horse and uncover his remarkable accomplishments.

John Horse took a bold stand against slavery, leading daring raids on plantations in Florida and liberating enslaved individuals. By burning down several plantations, he struck a blow against the oppressive system and helped dismantle slavery in the region. Horse's actions demonstrated his unwavering commitment to justice and freedom.

The Black Seminoles, including Horse, faced formidable opposition from the US Army, which sought to oppress and enslave them. Despite being outnumbered, they developed innovative guerrilla warfare tactics, utilizing their knowledge of the Florida swamps. By striking and retreating into the inaccessible swamps, they evaded capture and disrupted the plans of their adversaries.

Remarkably, the Black Seminoles managed to defeat much larger forces of the US military and slave owners, displaying remarkable resilience and strategic brilliance. Their determination and tenacity inspired others and proved that even in the face of overwhelming odds, freedom could be achieved.

Recognizing the strength and resilience of the Black Seminoles, the US government eventually made a deal with them. In 1838, John Horse and his people agreed to leave Florida and relocate to Oklahoma. There, Horse founded a Black town known as Wewoka, providing a safe haven for his community to rebuild their lives and preserve their culture.

Horse's influence extended beyond the United States. He and his men ventured to Mexico, where they protected the Mexican border from hostile Red Native American tribes. In exchange for their services, they received political protections and land grants from Mexico. During the border conflicts of the 1870s, Horse's leadership and military prowess enabled them to defeat the Texas Rangers, further solidifying their reputation as formidable fighters.

John Horse's exceptional leadership and military achievements establish him as one of the greatest unsung military leaders in American history.

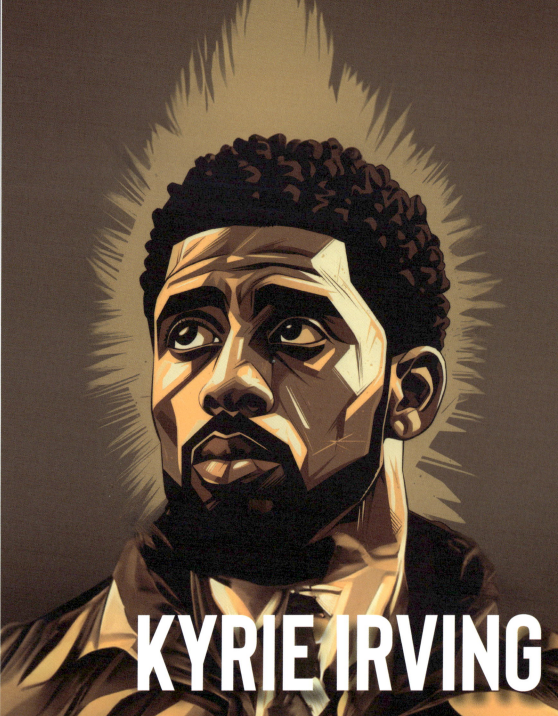

KYRIE IRVING
A Talented NBA Player and Advocate

Kyrie Irving, born on March 23, 1992, is a renowned professional basketball player known for his exceptional skills on the court and his dedication to social activism. Let's explore the inspiring journey of Kyrie Irving and his impact both on and off the basketball court.

Kyrie Irving's basketball career has been nothing short of impressive. He entered the NBA in 2011 and quickly made a name for himself with his incredible ball-handling skills and scoring ability. Throughout his career, he has played for various teams, displaying his talent and contributing to their success. His agility, quickness, and scoring prowess have earned him numerous accolades, including All-Star selections and an NBA championship.

Beyond his basketball achievements, Kyrie Irving has also used his platform to advocate for social justice and equality. He has been actively involved in various community initiatives, particularly those supporting the Black community. From providing scholarships to disadvantaged youth to organizing events that promote education and empowerment, Irving has consistently demonstrated his commitment to making a positive impact.

Irving's activism has extended beyond charitable efforts. He has fearlessly spoken out on issues of racial inequality, police brutality, and the importance of mental health. Through his actions and statements, he has encouraged open dialogue and raised awareness about important social issues affecting marginalized communities.

In his journey, Kyrie Irving has faced scrutiny and targeting from the NBA league and mainstream media for his views and actions. However, he has remained steadfast in his beliefs and continued to use his platform to amplify the voices of the oppressed. His resilience and determination serve as an inspiration to others, encouraging them to stand up for what they believe in and fight for justice.

PERCY JULIAN

(1899-1975): The Brilliant Foundational Black American Scientist

Percy Julian, born on April 11, 1899, in Montgomery Alabama was an exceptional Foundational Black American scientist who made groundbreaking contributions to the fields of chemistry and medicine.

Julian's journey began with his early education. He attended an all-Black high school where his teachers recognized his immense potential. With their encouragement and support, he excelled in science and mathematics, paving the way for his future scientific endeavors.

After high school, Julian attended DePauw University in Indiana, where he graduated as the valedictorian of his class. He went on to pursue advanced degrees at Harvard University. Despite facing racial barriers and prejudice, Julian persisted and earned his master's and doctoral degrees.

Throughout his career, Percy Julian made remarkable scientific innovations. He developed a way to synthesize physostigmine, a compound used in treating glaucoma, which was a major breakthrough in medicine. Julian's discoveries in the field of synthetic hormones also revolutionized medical science, leading to the development of important treatments for various conditions such as arthritis and asthma.

COLIN KAEPERNICK

Colin Kaepernick (born on November 3, 1987) is a former NFL player known not only for his athletic skills but also for his impactful activism.

Born in Milwaukee, Wisconsin, Kaepernick excelled in sports at an early age, particularly football. Kaepernick's talent on the field led him to play college football at the University of Nevada, where he became a star quarterback.

In 2011, Kaepernick was drafted into the NFL by the San Francisco 49ers. He quickly gained recognition for his exceptional skills, including his strong arm and ability to run. Kaepernick played a key role in leading his team to the Super Bowl in 2013, capturing the attention of fans worldwide.

However, it was Kaepernick's activism that made headlines and sparked a significant controversy. In 2016, he chose to take a knee during the national anthem before games to protest racial injustice and police brutality against Black Americans. This act of peaceful protest drew both support and criticism from people across the country.

Kaepernick's protest ignited a global conversation about social inequality and systemic racism. It sparked movements and inspired athletes, activists, and individuals from various backgrounds to speak out against injustice. Kaepernick's bold stance demonstrated the power of athletes to use their platform for social change.

Despite facing backlash and criticism, Kaepernick remained steadfast in his commitment to fighting for justice. He launched the Know Your Rights Camp, a youth empowerment initiative focused on education and self-empowerment for marginalized communities. Kaepernick's activism extended beyond football, as he dedicated his efforts to making a positive impact on society.

Colin Kaepernick's legacy is one of resilience and advocacy. His activism continues to influence discussions about race, equality, and the role of athletes in promoting social change.

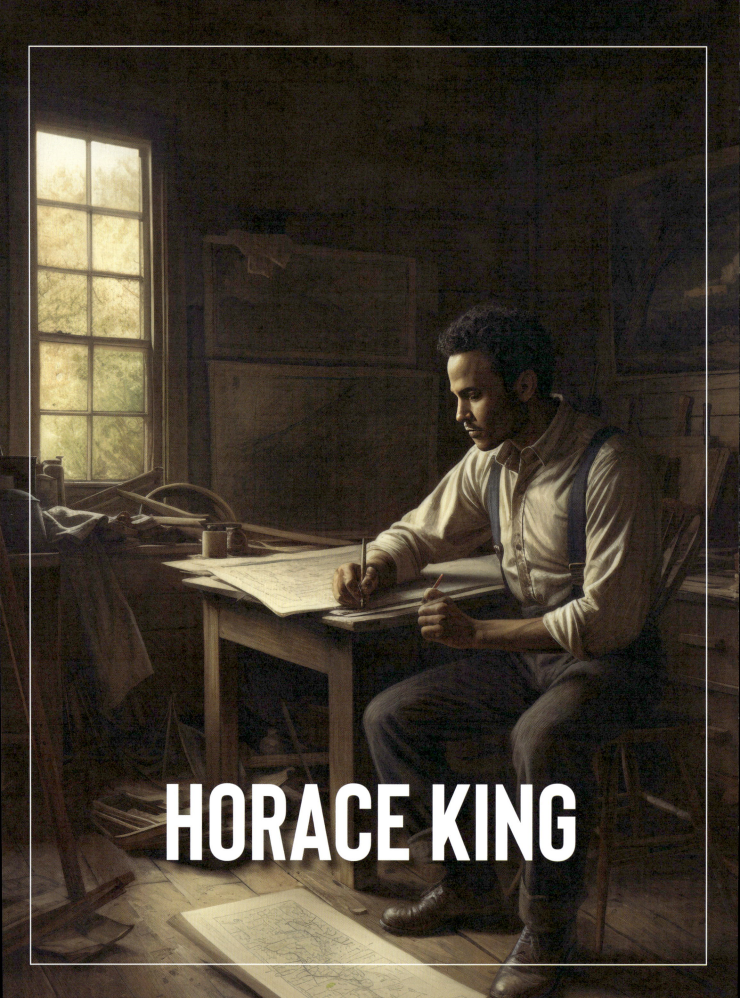

HORACE KING

(1807-1885): Enslaved Architect Who Built Bridges to Freedom

Horace King, born in 1807, was an enslaved architect whose remarkable skills and determination defied the restrictions of his time. Let's explore the life of Horace King, his extraordinary career, and the lasting impact of his architectural achievements.

Horace King was born into slavery in South Carolina. Despite the challenges he faced, he exhibited a natural talent for construction and an unwavering passion for architecture. His abilities caught the attention of John Godwin, a renowned architect who recognized King's potential and purchased him to work as a carpenter and builder.

King honed his skills and became renowned for his meticulous attention to detail and innovative designs. One of his greatest achievements was his contribution to bridge construction. King designed and constructed numerous bridges throughout the Southern United States, including the remarkable Hawkinsville Bridge over the Chattahoochee River in Georgia. These bridges not only connected communities but also facilitated trade and transportation, contributing to the region's growth and development.

King's architectural prowess extended beyond bridges. He was involved in designing and constructing various buildings and structures that still stand as testaments to his talent. Notable among his works were courthouses, churches, and public buildings. These structures not only served practical purposes but also showcased King's exceptional craftsmanship and enriched the communities in which they stood.

Despite his enslaved status, Horace King was able to earn money from his highly sought-after architectural skills. With his earnings, he eventually purchased his freedom, gaining independence that allowed him to continue his architectural pursuits and leave a lasting legacy.

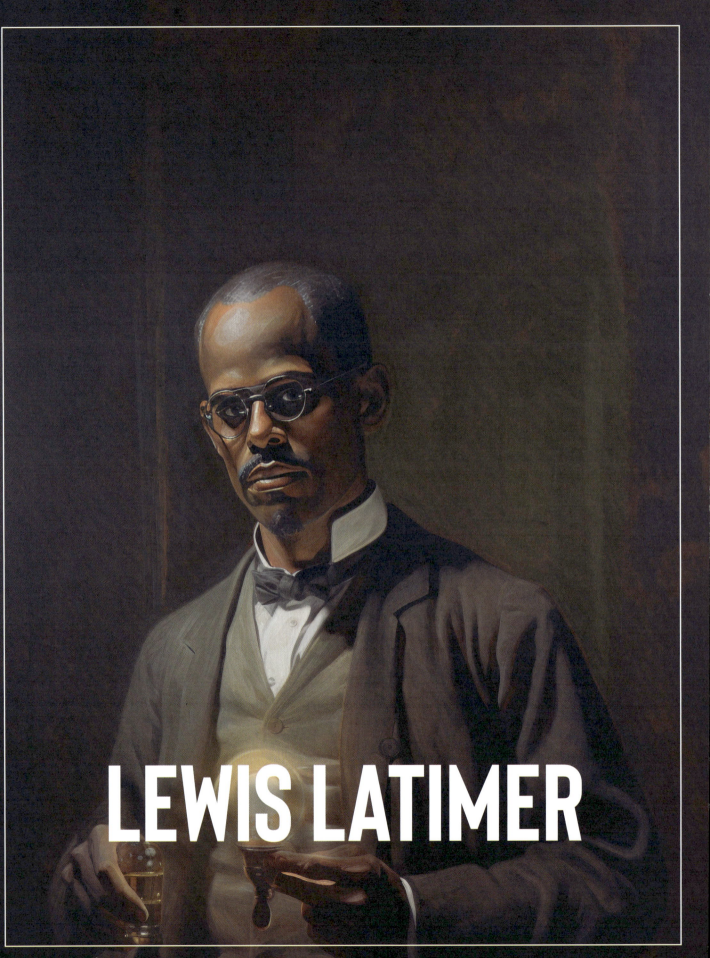

LEWIS LATIMER

(1848-1928): Foundational Black American Inventor and Pioneer of Electric Lighting

Lewis Latimer, born in Chelsea, Massachusetts, in 1848, was a brilliant inventor and pioneer in the field of electric lighting. From an early age, Latimer displayed a keen interest in science and engineering. Despite facing numerous challenges, including the racial prejudices of his time, he pursued his passion and became a self-taught inventor. Latimer's determination and talent caught the attention of notable inventors and engineers, opening doors for him in the field.

Latimer's most renowned invention was his improvement on the incandescent light bulb. While Thomas Edison is often credited with inventing the light bulb, many historians believe that Latimer's innovations played a crucial role in its development. Latimer's filament increased the efficiency and durability of the light bulb. His contributions were so significant that he is often regarded as the true inventor of the modern light bulb.

In addition to his work on the light bulb, Latimer authored the first book on electric lighting, entitled "Incandescent Electric Lighting." This publication provided valuable insights into electric lighting technology and its applications, establishing Latimer as a leading authority in the field.

Latimer's expertise was also sought after in the installation of public electric lights. He supervised the installation of electric lighting systems in major cities such as New York, Philadelphia, Montreal, and London. His knowledge and experience helped revolutionize urban landscapes, bringing forth a new era of safe and efficient lighting.

Beyond his contributions to electric lighting, Lewis Latimer held numerous other patents and inventions. He made significant advancements in areas such as water closet systems, electric railways, and ventilation devices, among others. His innovations continue to impact various industries to this day.

61

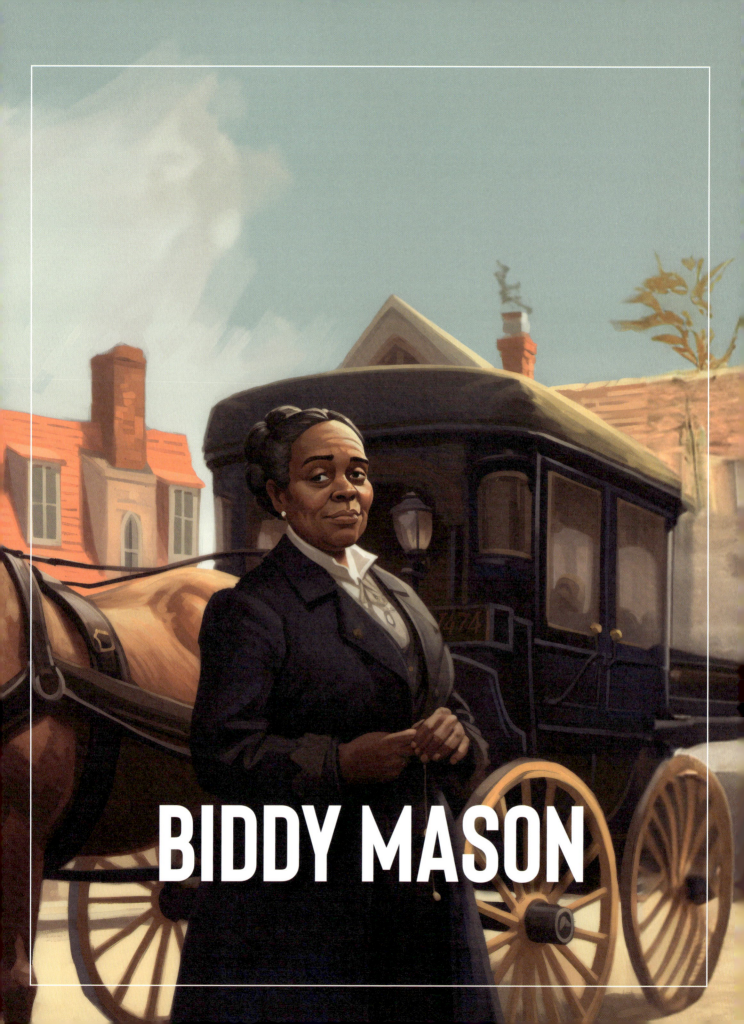

BIDDY MASON

(1818-1891): The Grandmother of Los Angeles

Biddy Mason was born into slavery on August 15, 1818, in Hancock County, Georgia. Her remarkable life journey took her from bondage to becoming one of the most influential figures in early Los Angeles

In the mid-1850s, Biddy Mason was brought to California by her owner. Even though slavery had been legally banned in California, many enslaved individuals remained in bondage due to informal slavery practices. Biddy's arrival in Los Angeles occurred during a time when the city was experiencing rapid growth and transformation.

Despite the challenges she faced, Biddy's resilience and determination shone through. In 1856, she seized an opportunity to fight for her freedom. Alongside other enslaved individuals, Biddy and her attorney argued that their extended residency in California made them eligible for emancipation under state law. The court ruled in their favor, granting them their freedom. This landmark case marked a significant step towards the fight against slavery.

With her newfound freedom, Biddy Mason embarked on a path of remarkable success. Through her hard work and business acumen, she became the wealthiest woman in California during her time. Biddy engaged in various business endeavors, including midwifery and nursing, and her skills were highly sought after in the growing community.

Biddy's real estate investments played a crucial role in her accumulation of wealth. She purchased valuable properties and land, making astute decisions that contributed to her financial success. Her business dealings extended beyond real estate, as she also ventured into livestock and other ventures.

Biddy Mason's influence and impact on early Los Angeles were profound. As one of the city's earliest Foundational Black American landowners, she played a pivotal role in shaping the community. Her success and philanthropy inspired others and contributed to the growth and development of early Los Angeles.

Biddy's philanthropic endeavors were significant. She used her wealth to help those in need, providing support to charitable causes and aiding the less fortunate. Biddy's generosity left an indelible mark on the city and exemplified her commitment to making a positive difference in the lives of others.

Today, Biddy Mason is often referred to as the "Grandmother of Los Angeles." This title reflects her enduring legacy as a trailblazer, a woman of strength, resilience, and determination.

TARIQ NASHEED
Documentarian and Activist

Tariq Nasheed is a prominent figure known for his thought-provoking documentary films, impactful books, and passionate activism.

Tariq Nasheed was born in Detroit, Michigan, and spent his childhood primarily in Birmingham, Alabama. These early geographic experiences exposed him to different aspects of Foundational Black American culture, giving him a deeper appreciation of its various nuances. However, it was during his most formative years in Los Angeles, California, that Nasheed was further influenced by the city's vibrant culture and diverse community, enriching his understanding and connection to the multifaceted tapestry of Foundational Black American heritage.

Nasheed later gained recognition for his groundbreaking documentary series, Hidden Colors. This film series explores the untold history of people of African and Foundational Black American descent, shedding light on their contributions and struggles throughout history. Hidden Colors has had a global impact, resonating with audiences around the world and sparking important conversations about Black history. It stands as one of the most successful Black history film series to date.

Beyond his work as a documentarian, Nasheed is also a New York Times best-selling author. His books offer unique insights into relationships, self-improvement, race and success. Nasheed's ability to connect with readers and share his perspectives has earned him a dedicated following.

Nasheed's commitment to preserving and sharing Black history is further demonstrated by his acquisition of the Hidden History Museum in Los Angeles. Located in the historic Jefferson Park area, once a prominent Black community, the museum serves as a space to educate and inspire visitors about the rich heritage and contributions of Black people throughout history.

OSMAN
The Feared Maroon Leader

Osman, a remarkable figure in history, stands as one of the renowned maroon leaders of the Great Dismal Swamp. While the exact details of his birth and death remain unknown, historians estimate that he was born in the late 18th century and passed away in the mid-19th century.

His story is intertwined with the backdrop of the Great Dismal Swamp, a unique and extraordinary place located in southeastern Virginia and northeastern North Carolina. The Great Dismal Swamp, spanning thousands of acres, became a sanctuary for enslaved individuals who sought freedom. Escaping from the harsh realities of slavery, these brave individuals transformed into maroons, forming communities within the depths of the swamp.

For hundreds of years, the Great Dismal Swamp served as a refuge for the maroons. Its dense vegetation, murky waters, and treacherous terrain made it a formidable obstacle for those attempting to enter the swamp. White society, unable to navigate the challenging landscape and aware of the maroons' adeptness in guerrilla warfare tactics, dared not venture into the depths of the swamp.

The Great Dismal Swamp emerged as the most successful safe haven for Black runaway freedom fighters during slavery. Its impenetrable nature, combined with the maroons' knowledge of the terrain, ensured their survival. This unique sanctuary remained unconquered and untouched by the forces of white society.

Osman was a figure of both respect and fear. Enslaved individuals were afraid to inform on him or other maroons, knowing that there would be severe consequences. Even the oppressor class held a deep sense of fear towards Osman and his maroon community.

The legacy of Osman and the maroons of the Great Dismal Swamp serves as a testament to the indomitable spirit of those who fought against the shackles of slavery.

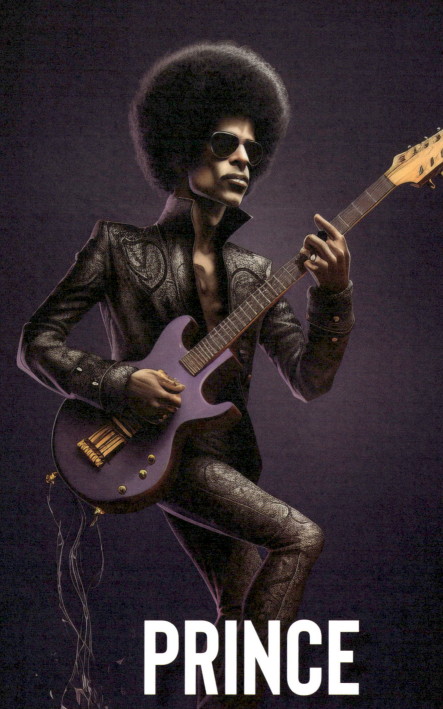

PRINCE ROGERS NELSON
(1958-2016): A Musical Visionary

Prince Rogers Nelson, known as Prince, was born on June 7, 1958, in Minneapolis, Minnesota, into a musical family. Immersed in various genres of music from an early age, Prince honed his extraordinary talents in singing, songwriting, and playing multiple instruments such as guitar, piano, and drums. Blending funk, rock, pop, and R&B, Prince's music captivated millions worldwide.

One of Prince's notable contributions was his unwavering support for ownership, particularly Black ownership, within the music industry. He recognized the unfair treatment often faced by artists, especially those from marginalized Black communities, and advocated for their right to control their music and receive fair compensation for their artistry.

Having witnessed the challenges artists confronted in a corporate-dominated industry, Prince was determined to challenge the status quo. He actively fought against exploitative practices and sought to empower artists to take control of their careers and demand fair treatment for their creative work.

One notable act of defiance was when Prince famously scribbled the word "Slave" on his face during television performances, symbolically representing his protest against the industry's oppressive practices.

His activism and dedication to creative control continue to resonate, reminding artists that they have the power to shape their own destinies and advocate for their rights.

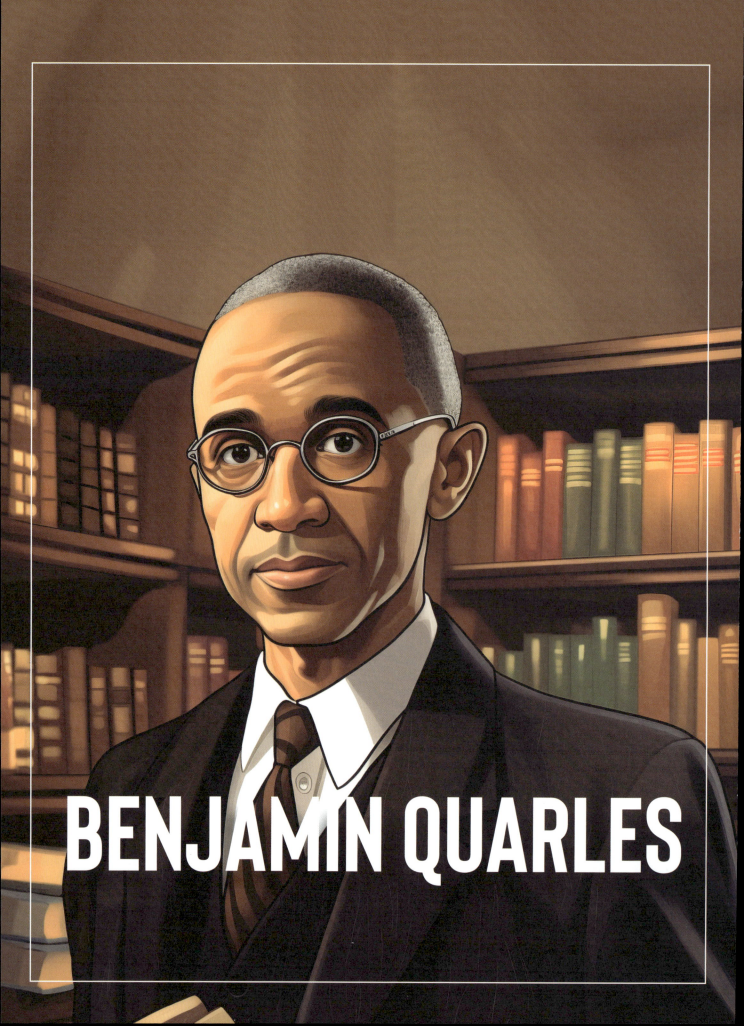

Q

BENJAMIN QUARLES
(1904-1996): Pioneering Historian

Benjamin Quarles was a renowned historian and author who made significant contributions to the history of Foundational Black Americans. Born in Boston, Massachusetts, Quarles excelled academically and eventually earned a bachelor's degree from Shaw University and a master's degree in history from the University of Wisconsin.

Quarles' work as a historian was groundbreaking and pivotal in shaping our understanding of the experiences of Foundational Black Americans. His research and writings focused on the struggles, achievements, and contributions of Black individuals in America.

One of Quarles' most significant works is his book "The Negro in the American Revolution," which examined the role and contributions of Foundational Black Americans during the American Revolutionary War. This book brought attention to the Black soldiers who fought for their freedom and the establishment of an independent nation, highlighting their bravery and dedication to the cause of liberty.

Another influential work by Quarles is "The Negro in the Making of America," a comprehensive account of the history of Foundational Black Americans from the early days of slavery to the Civil Rights Movement.

Quarles' thorough research and perceptive analysis established him as a renowned authority in the field of history. His works were meticulously crafted, drawing from primary sources, archives, and historical documents to provide a comprehensive and precise portrayal of the experiences of Foundational Black Americans.

BASS REEVES

BASS REEVES
(1838-1910): Legendary Lawman

Bass Reeves was an extraordinary lawman whose life was filled with remarkable achievements and inspiring acts of bravery. Born into slavery in Crawford County, Arkansas, Reeves faced many hardships during his early years. However, in a courageous act, he confronted his enslaver, who he believed was mistreating him, and successfully fought back. Fearing the consequences, Reeves escaped and sought refuge in Indian Territory, now known as Oklahoma.

In Oklahoma, Reeves found safety and companionship among the Black Seminoles, a community known for their resistance against oppression. The Black Seminoles provided him with protection and support as he embarked on a new chapter of his life. Reeves embraced their culture, learned their language, and honed his survival skills in the rugged wilderness.

Reeves's dedication and determination caught the attention of U.S. Marshal James Fagan, who appointed him as a deputy U.S. Marshal in 1875. This made Reeves one of the first Black lawmen in the American West. Reeves served in the Indian Territory and later in the Oklahoma Territory, where he became a renowned lawman, feared by outlaws and respected by the communities he served.

His career as a lawman was marked by numerous accomplishments. Reeves apprehended over 3,000 fugitives and brought them to justice, earning a reputation as one of the most successful lawmen of his time. His tracking abilities, sharpshooting skills, and knowledge of the territory made him an invaluable asset in capturing dangerous criminals.

Interestingly, it is believed that the character of the Lone Ranger, a popular fictional hero of the American West, was inspired by the legendary exploits of Bass Reeves. Reeves's extraordinary achievements and unwavering commitment to upholding the law closely parallel the adventures of the Lone Ranger, solidifying his place in Western folklore.

Bass Reeves's significance lies not only in his accomplishments but also in his pioneering role as a Black lawman in a predominantly white society. He defied the racial prejudices of the era and demonstrated that individuals of any background can excel in their chosen field. His legacy serves as a testament to courage, resilience, and the fight for justice.

DR. SEBI

(1933-2016): Holistic Health Pioneer

Alfredo Darrington Bowman, popularly known as Dr. Sebi, dedicated his life to promoting natural healing through herbal medicine. Born in Honduras, Dr. Sebi's early life was influenced by his grandmother, who taught him about the power of plants and their potential to support wellness.

As he grew older, Dr. Sebi became passionate about exploring the healing properties of herbs. He observed how certain plants and natural remedies could contribute to overall well-being and help the body restore its balance. Inspired by these observations, he embarked on a journey to study and understand herbal medicine more deeply.

Dr. Sebi gained recognition for his unique approach to healing, focusing on cleansing the body and restoring its natural state. Through a carefully curated diet and the use of specific herbs, he aimed to eliminate toxins, promote vitality, and support the body's self-healing abilities.

Many people sought Dr. Sebi's guidance and experienced positive outcomes from his methods. His approach involved personalized protocols tailored to individual needs, emphasizing the importance of nutrition and herbal remedies.

In an infamous AIDS case, Dr. Sebi claimed to have discovered a cure, attracting praise and skepticism. He successfully defended himself in legal battles, further solidifying his reputation as a legitimate healer.

Working with various individuals, including celebrities, Dr. Sebi emphasized the importance of consuming alkaline foods and avoiding acidic foods for maintaining a balanced and healthy body.

Dr. Sebi's life and work continue to inspire discussions about natural healing and holistic approaches to wellness. Dr. Sebi's dedication to exploring the healing power of nature encourages individuals to consider alternative approaches to well-being and make informed choices about their health.

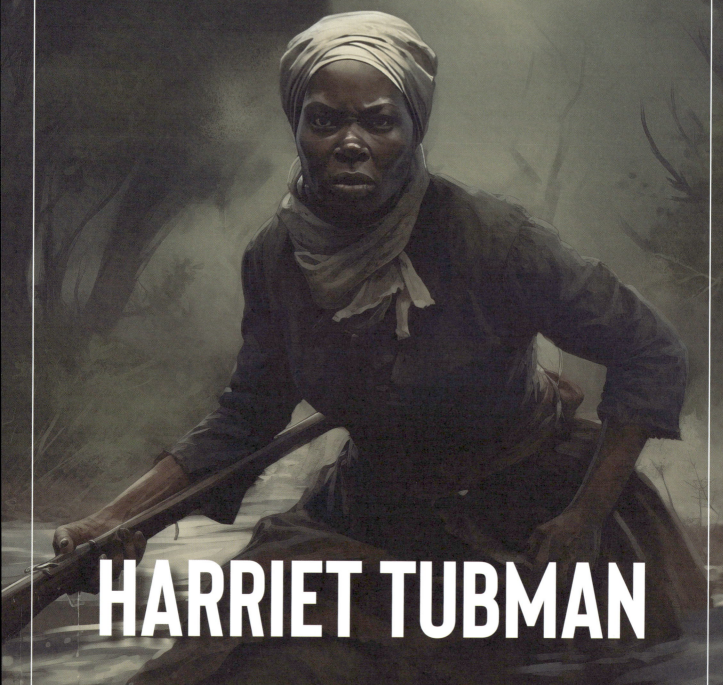

HARRIET TUBMAN

(c. 1822-1913): The Courageous Conductor of Freedom

Harriet Tubman was an influential figure in American history, known for her extraordinary courage and determination in the fight against slavery. Born into slavery in Maryland, Tubman experienced the harsh realities of bondage from an early age.

As a young woman, Tubman made the courageous decision to escape slavery and seek freedom. With unwavering determination, she embarked on a perilous journey along the Underground Railroad, a network of secret routes and safe houses that helped enslaved individuals escape to freedom. Tubman not only successfully liberated herself but also dedicated her life to helping others gain their freedom.

Tubman's efforts on the Underground Railroad were nothing short of remarkable. Over the course of many dangerous missions, she guided and led countless enslaved individuals to freedom, earning her the nickname "Moses" among those she rescued. Despite the constant threat of capture and the severe punishments that awaited both her and the fugitives she assisted, Tubman's commitment to justice and liberty remained unshaken.

During the Civil War, Tubman played a significant role as a Union spy, nurse, and scout. She served as a valuable source of intelligence, gathering critical information and helping to plan successful military operations. Tubman's contributions were widely recognized and appreciated by Union forces, who respected her strategic skills and her unwavering commitment to the cause of freedom.

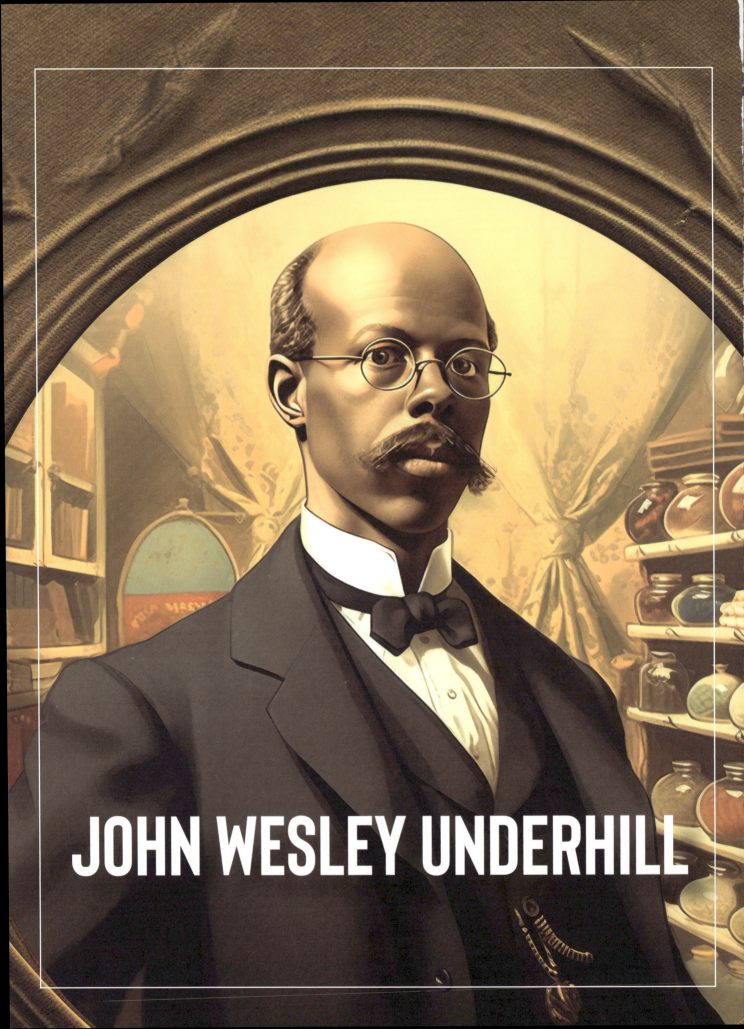

JOHN WESLEY UNDERHILL

The Mysterious Benefactor of Mays Landing

In the small town of Mays Landing, New Jersey, there once lived a man named John Wesley Underhill. He was a figure shrouded in mystery, seemingly appearing out of nowhere, but his impact on the community would be profound.

Mays Landing was a close-knit community in the early 20th century, home to around 2,500 residents. Among them, John Underhill stood alone as the only Black citizen of the town. Known as "Old John" in his later years, he was often seen as a recluse, living a quiet and solitary life.

Despite his reserved nature, Underhill had a modest candy store located near the downtown schools. Children would flock to his shop after school, eager to perform songs or dances they had learned, knowing they would be rewarded with penny candies. Underhill's store became a gathering place where talents were showcased, and moments of joy were shared.

In 1913, Underhill closed his beloved store, and the location was transformed into a Pool Room. This transition marked the end of an era, leaving many to wonder about the enigmatic figure who had brought so much joy to their lives.

When John Underhill passed away in 1925, the town of Mays Landing was astonished by his bequest. The reclusive man had quietly accumulated substantial wealth through years of hard work and frugal living. His generosity knew no bounds. Underhill had left behind a gift that would forever change the destiny of the town he had called home.

Underhill's estate revealed his true angelic nature. His liquidated assets provided his beloved community with an astounding gift of $100,000. It was a fortune that would echo through the generations, touching the lives of Mays Landing residents for years to come.

Underhill's instructions were clear and heartfelt. He wanted a gymnasium to be built as an addition to the new Mays Landing High School, offering a space for the physical well-being of the town's youth. He also desired the creation of playgrounds for children to enjoy, and a park adorned with a beautiful fountain and benches for families to gather and find solace.

Today, War Memorial Park on Main Street stands as a testament to John Wesley Underhill's mysterious and extraordinary legacy. Two plaques at the fountain bear his name, forever reminding the community of the generosity and kindness of the man who came seemingly out of nowhere, touched their lives, and left an everlasting impact.

John Wesley Underhill remains an enigmatic figure in the history of Mays Landing, a true guardian angel who turned the tides of fortune for his beloved community. His story continues to inspire and serves as a reminder that even the most mysterious among us can leave a profound mark on the world.

DENMARK VESEY
(1767-1822): Heroic Planner of Resistance

Denmark Vesey was born around 1767 on the island of St. Thomas, which was then a Danish colony in the Caribbean. When he was a teenager, he was brought to Charleston, South Carolina, as an enslaved person. Despite living in a world of oppression, Vesey never stopped dreaming of freedom.

After years of hard work and perseverance, Vesey won his freedom in a unique way. In 1800, he won a lottery ticket and used the prize money to purchase his freedom. This marked a turning point in Vesey's life, as he now had the opportunity to actively fight against the injustice of slavery.

Vesey found solace and strength in the African Methodist Episcopal Church, commonly known as Mother Emanuel. This church provided a safe space for enslaved individuals to gather, worship, and share their hopes and dreams of freedom. Vesey became a respected leader in the church and used it as a meeting place to plan a daring revolt against the oppressive system of slavery.

In the early 19th century, Vesey and a group of enslaved individuals meticulously planned a rebellion. Their goal was to seize control of Charleston, liberate the enslaved population, and establish a free society. The Mother Emanuel church became a crucial location for organizing and strategizing their efforts.

However, the planned revolt was discovered before it could take place. Vesey and his fellow conspirators were arrested, and Vesey was charged with treason. Throughout his trial, Vesey remained steadfast and resolute, refusing to provide any information that could endanger his comrades.

Sadly, Vesey's rebellion was unsuccessful, and he was executed in 1822. Although his revolt did not achieve its intended outcome, his bravery and determination continue to inspire people to this day. Vesey's actions played a significant role in raising awareness about the cruelty of slavery and the fight for freedom.

Denmark Vesey's story is a reminder of the power of courage and the importance of standing up against injustice. His legacy lives on as a symbol of resilience and determination.

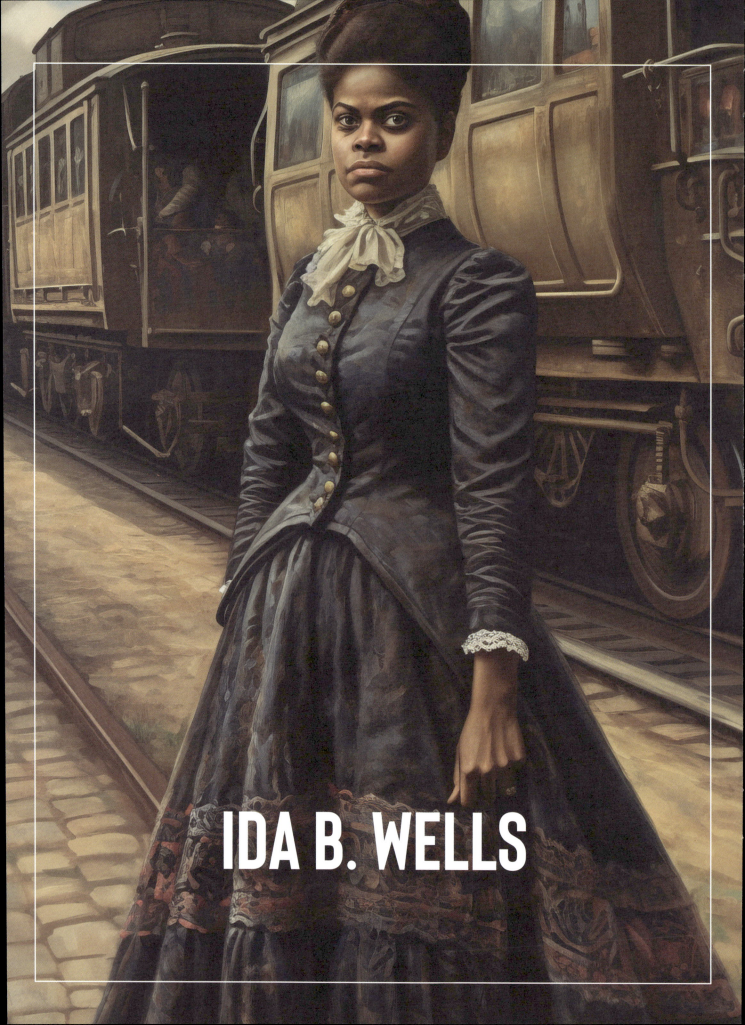

IDA B. WELLS

(1862-1931): Fierce Fighter for Freedom

Ida B. Wells was a fearless journalist, educator, and civil rights activist who dedicated her life to fighting for justice and equality for Foundational Black Americans. Her powerful voice and unwavering determination left an indelible mark on the history of the United States.

Born on July 16, 1862, in Holly Springs, Mississippi, during a time of deep racial inequality, Ida experienced the harsh realities of segregation from a young age. However, instead of succumbing to the oppression, she channeled her passion for justice into making a difference.

Ida's journey as a journalist began when she sued a train company in 1884 for forcefully removing her from a first-class train car due to her race. Although she did not win the case, it ignited her determination to expose and challenge racial injustice through her writing.

Her most significant contributions came in her tireless efforts to document and speak out against the brutal practice of lynching. Through her investigative reporting, Ida shed light on the horrifying acts of violence against Foundational Black

Americans and became a prominent voice against lynching. Her courageous writings brought national and international attention to this grave issue and spurred efforts to end this form of racial terrorism.

As the co-owner and editor of the Memphis Free Speech and Headlight newspaper, Ida fearlessly used her platform to advocate for the rights of Foundational Black Americans. She called for education and economic opportunities for black communities and urged them to resist oppression. Ida's bold stance challenged the status quo and inspired others to join the fight for justice and equality.

Despite facing numerous threats and acts of violence, Ida's determination remained unyielding. She traveled extensively, delivering powerful speeches and raising awareness about the injustices faced by Foundational Black Americans. Her advocacy work laid the foundation for civil rights organizations and served as a catalyst for change.

Ida B. Wells left a lasting legacy of courage, resilience, and a relentless pursuit of justice. Her unwavering dedication to documenting and challenging racial violence and discrimination paved the way for the civil rights movement and continues to inspire generations.

GRACE WISHER

GRACE WISHER

Grace Wisher (c. 1799-unknown): The Foundational Black American Girl Behind the American Flag

Grace Wisher, an enslaved girl, played a significant role in the creation of the modern American flag at a young age. Born around 1799, Grace lived during a time when slavery was prevalent in the United States.

At just 13 years old, Grace began working as an apprentice to Mary Pickersgill, a skilled flag maker in Baltimore, Maryland. Mary was commissioned by the United States government to sew a large flag for Fort McHenry. This flag was intended to be a symbol of national unity and pride.

Together, Grace and Mary and other Black American women worked diligently on the flag, carefully sewing each stripe and attaching the stars. The irony lies in the bittersweet paradox of Grace Wisher, an enslaved individual, skillfully stitching together a flag that would one day wave as a symbol of freedom, serving as a poignant reminder of the glaring contrast between her own bondage and the ideals it came to represent.

The completed flag, known as the Star-Spangled Banner, flew proudly above Fort McHenry during the War of 1812.

In September 1814, British forces attacked the fort, but the flag, sewn by Grace and Mary, withstood the relentless bombardment.

The resilience of the flag inspired Francis Scott Key to write a poem, which later became the national anthem of the United States, "The Star-Spangled Banner." Grace's contribution to the creation of this iconic flag symbolizes the strength and resilience of Foundational Black Americans in the face of adversity.

While the exact details of Grace Wisher's later life are unknown, her involvement in sewing the American flag remains a remarkable achievement. Her skill as a young seamstress and her dedication to creating a symbol of unity and freedom is an enduring legacy.

Recognizing the contributions of individuals like Grace Wisher highlights the importance of acknowledging the diverse history of the United States. It reminds us of the talent, perseverance, and resilience of Foundational Black Americans, whose efforts have left a lasting impact on the nation's history.

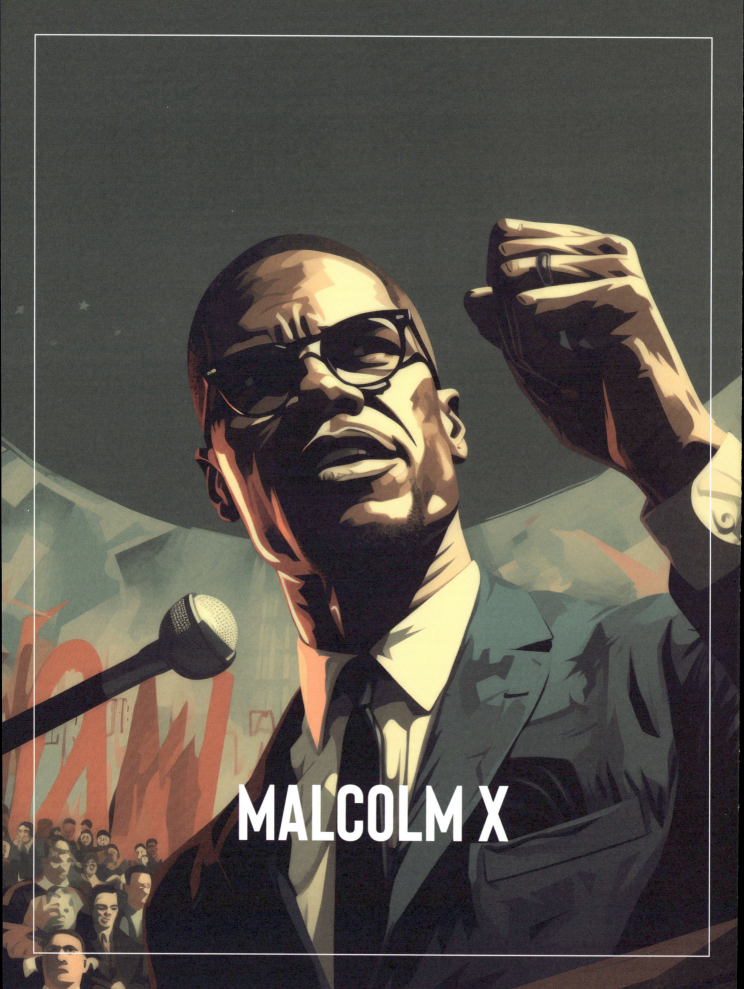

MALCOLM X

(1925-1965): Relentless Revolutionary

Malcolm X, born on May 19, 1925, in Omaha, Nebraska, was a prominent civil rights activist and an influential figure in the Black American struggle for equality. His early life was marked by significant challenges and experiences that shaped his later activism.

Growing up, Malcolm X faced racism and discrimination, witnessing firsthand the injustices faced by Black Americans. After his father's violent death and his family's subsequent struggles, Malcolm moved to Boston, Massachusetts, where he became involved in criminal activities. However, while serving time in prison, Malcolm underwent a transformative journey that would change the course of his life.

During his imprisonment, Malcolm X discovered the Nation of Islam, a religious and political movement advocating for Black self-determination. After his release from prison, he joined the Nation of Islam and adopted the surname "X" as a symbol of his lost identity. The X represented the unknown last name that had been taken from his ancestors during slavery.

Under the guidance of the Honorable Elijah Muhammad, the leader of the Nation of Islam, Malcolm X emerged as a powerful orator and an influential spokesperson for the organization. He preached about the importance of self-reliance, Black pride, and the necessity of addressing social and economic inequalities. His passionate speeches and charismatic presence attracted many followers.

Malcolm X's "By Any Means Necessary" approach to civil rights became a significant counterbalance to the nonviolent strategies advocated by other civil rights leaders. While others promoted peaceful protests and integration, Malcolm X argued for self-defense and highlighted the urgency of Black empowerment. His strong words and uncompromising stance resonated with many who were frustrated by the slow progress of the civil rights movement.

Malcolm X's legacy continues to inspire people around the world. His passionate advocacy for Black liberation, his unwavering commitment to truth and justice, and his willingness to challenge societal norms have made him an enduring symbol of courage and resilience in the fight against racism and inequality.

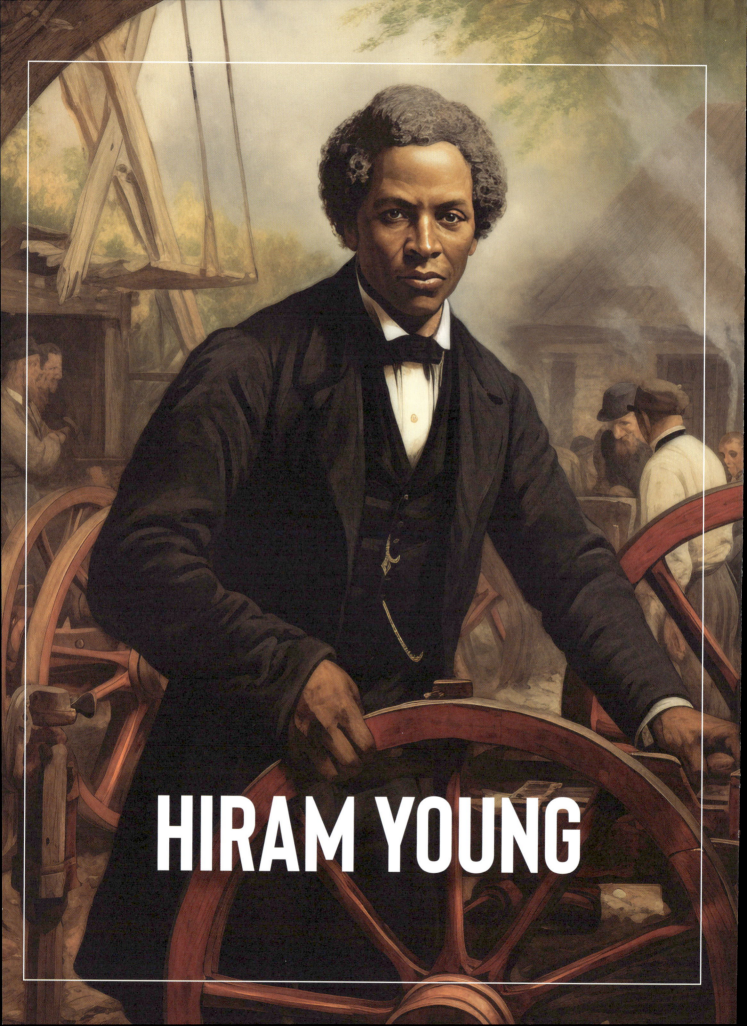

HIRAM YOUNG

(1812-1882): A Pioneer of Freedom and Success

Hiram Young, born in 1812, was an extraordinary individual who overcame the challenges of slavery to become one of the most accomplished wagon makers in the American West. His story is one of resilience, entrepreneurship, and a profound commitment to helping others.

Born into slavery as a Foundational Black American in Tennessee, Hiram Young faced the harsh realities of a system that denied freedom and opportunities to millions of people like him. However, he never lost hope and worked diligently to secure his freedom. Through meticulous saving, Young was able to accumulate the necessary funds to purchase his own emancipation in the early 1840s, gaining his independence and taking control of his own destiny.

Once free, Young embarked on a remarkable journey of self-discovery and determination. He honed his skills as a wagon maker and craftsman, dedicating himself to mastering his craft. Young's exceptional talent and commitment to excellence resulted in the production of wagons that were renowned for their superior quality and durability.

Word of Young's exceptional wagons spread like wildfire throughout the American West. Their sturdiness, attention to detail, and innovative designs set them apart from other wagons available at the time. Farmers, pioneers, and traders sought out Young's wagons for their reliability and ability to withstand the rugged terrain and demanding conditions of the frontier.

Young's reputation as a wagon maker soared, and demand for his wagons grew exponentially. His business flourished as customers recognized the unrivaled craftsmanship that went into each wagon. Hiram Young became synonymous with excellence, and his wagons were highly sought after by those who valued quality and reliability.

But Hiram Young's impact extended far beyond his wagon-making prowess. He used his success and wealth to uplift and empower others. Young, having experienced the hardships of slavery firsthand, empathized deeply with those still in bondage. He actively participated in efforts to assist enslaved individuals on their journey to freedom.

Throughout his life, Hiram Young remained committed to the well-being of his community and the fight for equality. His dedication to craftsmanship, coupled with his unwavering belief in the inherent worth and dignity of all individuals, made him an inspiration to those around him.

Z

ZIRYAB

(789-857): The Influential Moorish Innovator

Ziryab, whose name means "Blackbird" in Arabic, was a remarkable figure who left an indelible mark on Moorish Spain, also known as Al-Andalusia, during the 9th century. Born in 789 in Baghdad, Ziryab's journey took him from his homeland to the vibrant cultural melting pot of Moorish Spain.

During this period, the Moors, primarily composed of Black men, ventured into parts of Southern Europe and ruled for an impressive span of 700 years. It is important to note that many of the Moors were indeed Black, and the term "Moor" is believed to be derived from the Latin word "Maurus," meaning "Black."

Ziryab, known for his captivating voice and stunning appearance, quickly became a celebrity in Moorish Spain. He not only had a beautiful singing voice but was also a talented songwriter. Ziryab's contributions extended beyond music, as he introduced a multitude of cultural innovations that forever transformed Europe.

Ziryab revolutionized fashion in Moorish Spain and beyond. He introduced new clothing styles and trends, including seasonal fashion, that were adopted by the aristocracy and elite. Additionally, Ziryab brought the concept of personal hygiene to Europe by introducing toothpaste and proper grooming practices, which were previously unfamiliar to the region.

His influence extended to cuisine as well. Ziryab introduced the concept of a four-course meal, which included distinct courses for appetizers, main dishes, desserts, and beverages. This innovative culinary approach forever altered dining customs in Europe.

In the realm of music, Ziryab was a maestro. He played various instruments, including the oud, a stringed instrument similar to a lute, and introduced new musical styles and techniques. Ziryab's musical legacy resonated throughout Moorish Spain, inspiring generations of musicians and shaping the development of European music.

Ziryab's cultural contributions left an enduring legacy in Spain and Europe for centuries to come. His impact transcended borders and influenced fashion, grooming, cuisine, and music. His teachings and innovations were passed down through generations, contributing to the rich tapestry of European culture.